BAKING with my BESTIE

Publications International, Ltd.

ISBN: 978-1-63938-837-0

Manufactured in China.

8 7 6 5 4 3 2 1

Let's get social!
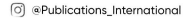 @Publications_International
@PublicationsInternational
www.pilbooks.com

TABLE of CONTENTS

CUPCAKE CUTIES

Peanut Butter and Jelly Cupcakes

makes 22 cupcakes

CUPCAKES

- 1 package (about 15 ounces) yellow cake mix, plus ingredients to prepare mix
- 2 cups strawberry jelly

FROSTING

- ³/₄ cup creamy peanut butter
- ¹/₂ cup (1 stick) butter, softened
- 2 cups powdered sugar
- ¹/₂ teaspoon vanilla
- ¹/₄ cup milk

1 Preheat oven to 350°F. Line 22 standard (2¹/₂-inch) muffin cups with paper baking cups.

2 Prepare cake mix according to package directions. Spoon batter evenly into prepared muffin cups. Bake 18 to 20 minutes or until toothpick inserted into centers comes out clean. Cool in pans 5 minutes. Remove to wire racks; cool completely.

3 Place jelly in pastry bag fitted with small round tip. Insert tip into tops of cupcakes; squeeze bag gently to fill centers with jelly.

4 For frosting, beat peanut butter and butter in large bowl with electric mixer at medium speed until smooth. Add powdered sugar and vanilla; beat at low speed until crumbly. Gradually add milk, beating until creamy; beat at medium-high speed until light and fluffy. Pipe or spread onto cupcakes.

Toasted Meringue Cupcakes
makes 9 jumbo cupcakes

CUPCAKES

1³/₄ cups all-purpose flour

1¹/₄ cups sugar

2 teaspoons baking powder

¹/₂ teaspoon salt

³/₄ cup vegetable oil

³/₄ cup milk

3 eggs

1¹/₂ teaspoons vanilla

8 ounces semisweet chocolate, melted and cooled slightly

MERINGUE

4 egg whites, at room temperature

6 tablespoons sugar

1 Preheat oven to 350°F. Line 9 jumbo (3¹/₂-inch) muffin cups with paper baking cups.

2 Whisk flour, 1¹/₄ cups sugar, baking powder and salt in large bowl. Add oil, milk, eggs and vanilla; beat with electric mixer at medium speed 2 minutes or until well blended. Stir in melted chocolate until well blended. Spoon batter into prepared muffin cups, filling two-thirds full.

3 Bake 25 minutes or until toothpick inserted into centers comes out clean. Cool in pans 5 minutes. Remove to wire rack; cool completely.

4 Increase oven temperature to 375°F. For meringue, whip egg whites in large bowl with electric mixer at high speed until soft peaks form. Gradually add 6 tablespoons sugar, beating until stiff peaks form. Pipe or spread meringue on cupcake.

5 Place cupcakes on baking sheet. Bake 5 minutes or until peaks of meringue are golden.

Sealed with a Kiss Cupcakes

makes 12 cupcakes

1 cup white or pink candy melting discs or chopped white almond bark

Hot pink or red decorating sugar

1¼ cups all-purpose flour

1½ teaspoons baking powder

1 teaspoon baking soda

½ teaspoon salt

1 cup granulated sugar

½ cup plus ¾ teaspoon vegetable oil, divided

2 eggs

½ cup milk

1½ cups semisweet chocolate chips

Chocolate sprinkles

1 Draw at least 12 (2-inch) sets of lips on sheet of parchment paper with marker. Turn paper over; place on baking sheet. (You should be able to see outlines of lips through paper.) Melt candy discs according to package directions; place in plastic squeeze bottle or piping bag fitted with small round tip. Pipe lips on parchment paper using outlines as guide; sprinkle immediately with decorating sugar. Let stand until set.

2 Preheat oven to 350°F. Line 12 standard (2½-inch) muffin cups with paper baking cups.

3 Whisk flour, baking powder, baking soda and salt in small bowl. Combine granulated sugar, ½ cup oil and eggs in large bowl; whisk until well blended. Add flour mixture and milk; stir just until blended. Spoon batter evenly into prepared muffin cups.

4 Bake 18 to 20 minutes or until toothpick inserted into centers comes out clean. Cool in pan 5 minutes. Remove to wire rack; cool completely.

5 Combine chocolate chips and remaining ¾ teaspoon oil in medium microwavable bowl. Microwave on HIGH at 30-second intervals, stirring after each interval, until melted and smooth.

6 Place chocolate sprinkles in shallow bowl. Dip cupcakes in chocolate, then in sprinkles. Arrange lips on cupcakes. Let stand until set.

CUPCAKE CUTIES

Kittycakes
makes 22 cupcakes

2¹/₄ cups all-purpose flour

1 tablespoon baking powder

¹/₂ teaspoon salt

1¹/₂ cups sugar

¹/₂ cup (1 stick) butter, softened

4 egg whites

2 teaspoons vanilla

1 cup milk

White and pink candy wafers, black string licorice, pink heart decors and chocolate-covered sunflower seeds or mini candy-coated chocolate pieces

1 container (16 ounces) white frosting

Black food coloring

Black decorating icing

1 Preheat oven to 350°F. Line 22 standard (2¹/₂-inch) muffin cups with paper baking cups. Whisk flour, baking powder and salt in medium bowl.

2 Beat sugar and butter in large bowl with electric mixer at medium speed until fluffy. Add egg whites one at a time, beating well after each addition. Add vanilla; beat until blended. Add flour mixture alternately with milk, beating at low speed after each addition. Spoon batter into prepared muffin cups, filling two-thirds full.

3 Bake 18 to 20 minutes or until toothpick inserted into centers comes out clean. Cool in pans 5 minutes. Remove to wire racks; cool completely.

4 Cut candy wafers into triangles for ears. Cut licorice into 1-inch lengths for whiskers. (Cut licorice strings in half lengthwise for thinner whiskers.)

5 Reserve ¹/₂ cup frosting in small bowl. Place remaining frosting in medium microwavable bowl. Microwave on HIGH about 10 seconds or until very soft but not completely melted. Dip tops of cupcakes in frosting to coat; let stand until set.

6 Tint reserved frosting desired shade of gray with black food coloring. Place frosting in piping bag fitted with small round tip; pipe frosting on tops and sides of cupcakes. Place wafer ears and licorice whiskers on cupcakes. Attach sunflower seeds for eyes and heart decors for noses. Pipe mouths and pupils with decorating icing.

Bright Stripes Cupcakes
makes 20 cupcakes

1 package (about 15 ounces) white cake mix

1 cup sour cream

3 eggs

½ cup vegetable oil

Gel food coloring (4 colors)

1 container (16 ounces) white or cream cheese frosting

Mini rainbow candy-coated chocolate chips

1 Preheat oven to 325°F. Line 20 standard (2½-inch) muffin cups with white paper baking cups.

2 Beat cake mix, sour cream, eggs and oil in large bowl with electric mixer at low speed 30 seconds. Beat at medium speed 2 minutes or until well blended. Divide batter evenly among four medium bowls. Deeply tint batter in each bowl desired colors.

3 Spoon one color of batter into each prepared cup (about 2 teaspoons); spread batter to edge of cup with back of spoon or dampened fingers. Top with second color of batter, making sure to completely cover first layer. Repeat with remaining two colors of batter.

4 Bake 18 to 20 minutes or until toothpick inserted into centers comes out clean. Cool in pans 5 minutes. Remove to wire racks; cool completely.

5 Frost cupcakes; decorate with rainbow chocolate chips.

~•◦ **T • I • P** ◦•~

*Use as few or as many colors as you like for the rainbow layers
and adjust the amount of batter in each cup accordingly. For faster
layering of the different color batters, place each color batter into a
disposable piping bag or resealable food storage bag with one corner
cut off and pipe the layers into muffin cups instead of using a spoon.*

Sweet and Salty Cupcakes

makes 12 cupcakes

CUPCAKES

1¼ cups all-purpose flour

1 cup sugar

⅓ cup unsweetened Dutch process cocoa powder

1 teaspoon baking soda

½ teaspoon baking powder

½ teaspoon salt

½ cup buttermilk

½ cup coffee

¼ cup vegetable oil

1 egg

½ teaspoon vanilla

FROSTING AND TOPPINGS

1 cup semisweet chocolate chips

½ cup whipping cream

¾ cup honey roasted peanuts, coarsely chopped

¾ cup coarsely chopped pretzels

¼ to ½ cup caramel topping

1 Preheat oven to 350°F. Line 12 standard (2½-inch) muffin cups with paper baking cups.

2 Whisk flour, sugar, cocoa, baking soda, baking powder and salt in large bowl. Whisk buttermilk, coffee, oil, egg and vanilla in medium bowl until blended. Add to flour mixture; stir until well blended. Spoon batter evenly into prepared muffin cups.

3 Bake 18 to 20 minutes or until toothpick inserted into centers comes out clean. Cool cupcakes in pan 5 minutes. Remove to wire rack; cool completely.

4 For frosting, place chocolate chips in medium heatproof bowl. Bring cream to a simmer in small saucepan over medium heat; pour over chocolate chips. Let stand 5 minutes, then stir until blended and smooth. Set ganache aside about 20 minutes to thicken.

5 Dip tops of cupcake in ganache; return to wire rack. Sprinkle with peanuts and pretzels. Drizzle with caramel topping just before serving.

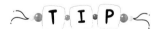
T · I · P

These cupcakes are best served the day they are made. To get ahead, bake the cupcakes the day before and add the frosting and toppings just before serving. The toppings will get soggy if they sit on the cupcakes too long.

Mini Doughnut Cupcakes
makes 60 mini cupcakes

1 cup sugar

1½ teaspoons ground cinnamon

1 package (about 15 ounces) yellow or white cake mix, plus ingredients to prepare mix

1 tablespoon ground nutmeg

1 Preheat oven to 350°F. Grease and flour 60 mini (1¾-inch) muffin cups. Combine sugar and cinnamon in large bowl; set aside.

2 Prepare cake mix according to package directions; stir in nutmeg. Spoon batter into prepared muffin cups, filling two-thirds full.

3 Bake 12 minutes or until lightly browned and toothpick inserted into centers comes out clean.

4 Remove cupcakes from pans. Roll warm cupcakes in sugar mixture until completely coated. Serve warm.

⁓•T•I•P•⁓

Save any remaining sugar mixture to sprinkle on toast and pancakes.

CUPCAKE CUTIES

Cherry Pink Cupcakes

makes 12 cupcakes

CUPCAKES

- 1 jar (10 ounces) maraschino cherries with stems
- 1¼ cups all-purpose flour
- 1½ teaspoons baking powder
- ½ teaspoon salt
- 1 cup granulated sugar
- 2 eggs
- ½ cup vegetable oil
- ½ cup milk
- 1 teaspoon vanilla

FROSTING

- 1 cup (2 sticks) butter, softened
- 4 cups powdered sugar
- 2½ tablespoons reserved cherry juice

1 Preheat oven to 350°F. Line 12 standard (2½-inch) muffin cups with paper baking cups. Drain cherries reserving juice for frosting. Reserve 12 cherries for garnish; stem and chop remaining cherries and squeeze out excess moisture between layers of paper towels. Spread cherries on paper towels to drain; set aside.

2 Whisk flour, baking powder and salt in medium bowl. Beat granulated sugar and eggs in large bowl with electric mixer at medium speed 5 minutes or until very pale and fluffy. Gradually beat in flour mixture at low speed. Add oil, milk and vanilla; beat 1 minute or until smooth. Stir in chopped cherries. Spoon batter evenly into prepared muffin cups.

3 Bake 18 to 20 minutes or until toothpick inserted into centers come out clean. Cool in pan on wire rack 5 minutes. Remove from pan; cool completely.

4 For frosting, beat butter in large bowl with electric mixer at medium speed until creamy. Gradually add powdered sugar at low speed. Add reserved cherry juice; beat at medium-high speed until fluffy. Fit piping bag with large star tip; fill with frosting. Pipe frosting in swirls on cupcakes. Garnish with reserved cherries.

Espresso Truffle Cupcakes
makes 24 cupcakes

GANACHE FROSTING

12 ounces bittersweet chocolate, chopped

1$\frac{1}{2}$ cups plus 3 tablespoons whipping cream, divided

2 tablespoons butter, cut into pieces

1$\frac{1}{2}$ teaspoons vanilla

CUPCAKES

2 cups all-purpose flour

1 teaspoon baking soda

$\frac{1}{2}$ teaspoon salt

$\frac{1}{2}$ cup unsweetened cocoa powder

1 tablespoon espresso powder*

$\frac{2}{3}$ cup boiling water

4 ounces bittersweet chocolate, finely chopped

$\frac{3}{4}$ cup (1$\frac{1}{2}$ sticks) butter, softened

1$\frac{1}{2}$ cups sugar

4 eggs

2 teaspoons vanilla

1 cup sour cream

*Or substitute instant coffee granules.

1 For frosting, place 12 ounces chocolate in food processor. Bring 1$\frac{1}{2}$ cups cream and 2 tablespoons butter to a simmer in small saucepan over medium-high heat. With motor running, slowly add hot cream mixture through feed tube; process about 4 minutes or until smooth and thickened. Stir in remaining 3 tablespoons cream and 1$\frac{1}{2}$ teaspoons vanilla. Transfer frosting to medium bowl. Press plastic wrap directly on surface; let stand about 3 hours or until thick and spreadable.

2 Preheat oven to 350°F. Line 24 standard (2$\frac{1}{2}$-inch) muffin cups with paper baking cups. Whisk flour, baking soda and salt in small bowl.

3 Combine cocoa and espresso powder medium bowl. Add boiling water; whisk until cocoa is dissolved. Add 4 ounces chocolate; whisk until melted.

4 Beat butter and sugar in large bowl with electric mixer at medium speed until light and fluffy. Add eggs one at a time, beating well after each addition. Add vanilla and chocolate mixture; mix well. Add flour mixture alternately with sour cream, mixing at low speed just until blended after each addition. Spoon batter into prepared muffin cups, filling two-thirds full.

5 Bake 18 to 20 minutes or until toothpick inserted in centers comes out clean. Cool in pans 5 minutes. Remove to wire rack; cool completely.

6 Place ganache frosting in piping bag fitted with medium star tip. Insert tip 1 inch into top of cupcake and squeeze until top begins to swell slightly. Decorate cupcakes with remaining frosting.

Salted Caramel Cupcakes

makes 12 cupcakes

CUPCAKES

1¹/₂ cups all-purpose flour

1 teaspoon baking powder

¹/₂ teaspoon salt

1 cup packed brown sugar

¹/₂ cup (1 stick) butter, softened

2 eggs

1 teaspoon vanilla

¹/₂ cup buttermilk

FROSTING

¹/₂ cup granulated sugar

2 tablespoons water

¹/₄ cup whipping cream

¹/₂ teaspoon salt

1 cup (2 sticks) butter, softened

2¹/₂ cups powdered sugar

Flaky sea salt

1 Preheat oven to 325°F. Line 12 standard (2¹/₂-inch) muffin cups with paper baking cups. Whisk flour, baking powder and ¹/₂ teaspoon salt in small bowl.

2 Beat brown sugar and ¹/₂ cup butter in large bowl with electric mixer at medium speed until fluffy. Add eggs and vanilla; beat until well blended. Add flour mixture and buttermilk; beat just until combined. Spoon batter evenly into prepared muffin cups.

3 Bake 20 to 25 minutes or until toothpick inserted into centers comes out clean. Cool in pan 5 minutes. Remove to wire rack; cool completely.

4 For frosting, heat granulated sugar and water in heavy medium saucepan over medium-high heat; cook without stirring until medium to dark amber in color. Remove from heat; carefully stir in cream and ¹/₂ teaspoon salt (mixture will foam). Cool 15 minutes.

5 Beat 1 cup butter and caramel mixture in large bowl with electric mixer at medium-high speed until well blended. Add powdered sugar; beat until thick and creamy. (If frosting is too soft, refrigerate 10 minutes before piping or spreading on cupcakes.) Pipe or spread frosting on cupcakes; sprinkle lightly with flaky salt.

Butterfly Cupcakes

makes 24 cupcakes

1 package (about 15 ounces) cake mix, any flavor, plus ingredients to prepare mix

1 container (16 ounces) white frosting

Blue and green food coloring

Colored sugar

Candy-coated chocolate pieces

Red string licorice, cut into 4-inch pieces

1 Preheat oven to 350°F. Spray 24 standard (2½-inch) muffin cups with nonstick cooking spray.

2 Prepare cake mix according to package directions. Spoon batter into prepared muffin cups, filling two-thirds full.

3 Bake 18 to 20 minutes or until toothpick inserted into centers comes out clean. Cool in pans 5 minutes. Remove to wire racks; cool completely.

4 Divide frosting between two small bowls; tint desired colors.

5 Cut cupcakes in half vertically. Place halves together, cut sides out, to resemble butterfly wings. Frost cupcakes; decorate with colored sugar and chocolate pieces. Snip each end of licorice pieces to form antennae; place in center of each cupcake.

Pumpkin Spice Cupcakes

makes 24 cupcakes

CUPCAKES

- 3 cups all-purpose flour
- 1 tablespoon baking powder
- 2 teaspoons ground cinnamon
- 1$\frac{1}{2}$ teaspoons baking soda
- $\frac{1}{2}$ teaspoon salt
- $\frac{1}{4}$ teaspoon ground allspice
- $\frac{1}{4}$ teaspoon ground nutmeg
- $\frac{1}{8}$ teaspoon ground ginger
- 1$\frac{1}{2}$ cups sugar
- $\frac{3}{4}$ cup (1$\frac{1}{2}$ sticks) butter, softened
- 3 eggs
- 1 can (15 ounces) pumpkin purée
- 1 cup buttermilk

FROSTING

- $\frac{3}{4}$ cup (1$\frac{1}{2}$ sticks) butter, softened
- 3 tablespoons maple syrup
- 2 tablespoons milk
- $\frac{1}{2}$ teaspoon vanilla
- 3$\frac{1}{2}$ cups powdered sugar
- Colored decors or sugar (optional)

1 Preheat oven to 350°F. Line 24 standard (2$\frac{1}{2}$-inch) muffin cups with paper baking cups. Whisk flour, baking powder, cinnamon, baking soda, salt, allspice, nutmeg and ginger in medium bowl.

2 Beat sugar and $\frac{3}{4}$ cup butter in large bowl with electric mixer at medium speed 3 minutes or until light and fluffy. Add eggs one at a time, beating well after each addition. Combine pumpkin and buttermilk in medium bowl; mix well. Alternately add flour mixture and pumpkin mixture, mixing at low speed just until blended after each addition. Spoon batter into prepared muffin cups, filling two-thirds full.

3 Bake 18 to 20 minutes or until toothpick inserted into centers comes out clean. Cool in pans 5 minutes. Remove to wire racks; cool completely.

4 For frosting, beat $\frac{3}{4}$ cup butter in large bowl with electric mixer at medium speed until creamy. Add maple syrup, milk and $\frac{1}{2}$ teaspoon vanilla; beat until well blended. Gradually add powdered sugar at low speed. Beat at medium-high speed until light and fluffy. Pipe or spread onto cupcakes. Sprinkle with decors, if desired.

Deluxe Chocolate Cookies
makes about 20 (4-inch) cookies

2 cups all-purpose flour

$^1/_3$ cup unsweetened cocoa powder

1 teaspoon baking soda

$^1/_2$ teaspoon salt

$1^1/_3$ cups packed brown sugar

1 cup (2 sticks) butter, softened

2 eggs

2 teaspoons vanilla

1 cup candy-coated chocolate pieces

1 cup dried cranberries, dried cherries and/or raisins

$^3/_4$ cup salted peanuts, chopped

1 Preheat oven to 350°F. Whisk flour, cocoa, baking soda and salt in medium bowl.

2 Beat brown sugar and butter in large bowl with electric mixer at medium speed until light and fluffy. Add eggs and vanilla; beat until well blended. Gradually add flour mixture; beat at low speed until blended. Stir in chocolate pieces, cranberries and peanuts.

3 Drop dough by $^1/_4$ cupfuls 3 inches apart onto ungreased cookie sheets. Flatten slightly with fingertips.

4 Bake 13 to 15 minutes or until almost set. Cool on cookie sheets 2 minutes. Remove to wire racks; cool completely.

Chocolate Chip Confetti Drops
makes 2 dozen cookies

1¼ cups all-purpose flour

½ teaspoon baking soda

½ teaspoon salt

½ cup (1 stick) butter, softened

½ cup granulated sugar

¼ cup packed brown sugar

1 egg

1 teaspoon vanilla

1 cup semisweet chocolate chips

⅓ cup rainbow sprinkles, plus additional for garnish

1 Preheat oven to 350°F. Line cookie sheets with parchment paper or lightly grease. Whisk flour, baking soda and salt in medium bowl.

2 Beat butter, granulated sugar and brown sugar in large bowl with electric mixer at medium speed until light and fluffy. Add egg and vanilla; beat until well blended. Add flour mixture; beat at low speed just until blended. Stir in chocolate chips and ⅓ cup sprinkles.

3 Shape rounded tablespoonfuls of dough into balls; dip tops in additional sprinkles. Place 2 inches apart onto prepared cookie sheets.

4 Bake 10 to 12 minutes or until edges are lightly browned. Cool on cookie sheets 1 minute. Remove to wire rack; cool completely.

NOTE: The dough can be made two days in advance. Store it in an airtight container or wrapped tightly in plastic wrap in the refrigerator.

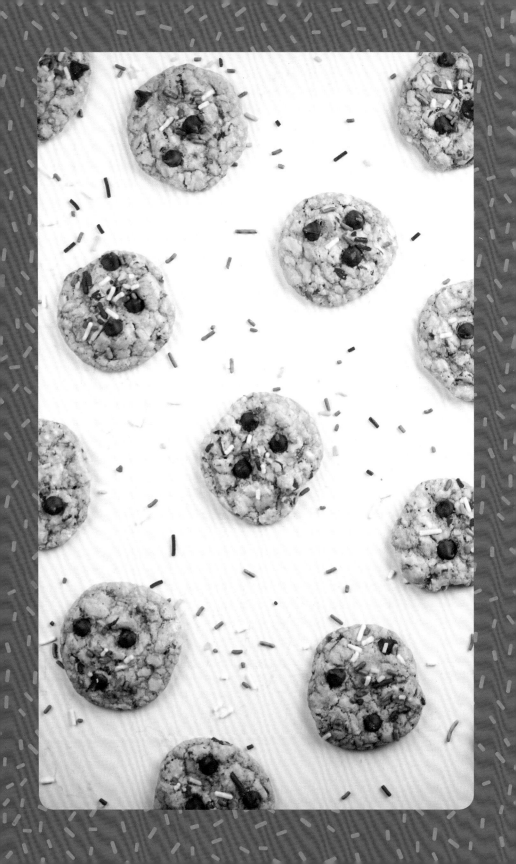

Toffee Latte Bars

makes 2 to 3 dozen bars

1½ cups all-purpose flour

¼ cup powdered sugar or granulated sugar

½ teaspoon salt

¾ cup (1½ sticks) cold butter, cut into small pieces

2 teaspoons instant coffee granules

1 teaspoon hot water

1 can (14 ounces) sweetened condensed milk

1 egg

1 teaspoon vanilla

1 package (8 ounces) toffee baking bits

1 cup chopped walnuts or white chocolate chips

2 cups large coconut flakes *or* 1 cup shredded coconut

1 Preheat oven to 350°F. Line 13×9-inch baking pan with parchment paper.

2 Combine flour, powdered sugar and salt in large bowl. Cut in butter with pastry blender or fingertips until mixture resembles coarse crumbs. Press into prepared pan. Bake 15 minutes or until lightly browned around edges.

3 Meanwhile, dissolve coffee granules in hot water in large bowl. Add sweetened condensed milk, egg and vanilla; whisk until well blended. Stir in toffee bits and nuts. Pour over crust; sprinkle with coconut.

4 Bake 25 minutes or until filling is set and coconut is toasted. Cool completely in pan on wire rack. Lift from pan using parchment; cut into bars.

Rainbow Sandwich Cookies
makes about 5 dozen cookies

COOKIES

1 cup (2 sticks) butter, softened

³/₄ cup granulated sugar, divided

¹/₃ cup whipping cream

1 teaspoon vanilla

¹/₄ teaspoon salt

2 cups all-purpose flour

FILLING

1¹/₄ cups (2¹/₂ sticks) butter, softened

4 cups powdered sugar

2 to 4 tablespoons whipping cream

1 teaspoon vanilla

Pinch of salt

Gel or liquid food coloring: red, orange, yellow, green, blue and purple

1 Beat 1 cup butter and ¹/₂ cup granulated sugar in large bowl with electric mixer at medium speed 3 minutes or until well blended. Add cream, vanilla and salt; beat until smooth and well blended. Gradually add flour at low speed, beating just until blended. Shape dough into two discs; wrap in plastic wrap. Refrigerate 1 hour or until firm.

2 Preheat oven to 350°F. Line cookie sheets with parchment paper or lightly grease. Working with one disc at a time, roll out dough on lightly floured surface to ¹/₈-inch thickness. Cut with 1¹/₂- to 2-inch round cutter; place cutouts on prepared cookie sheets. Sprinkle tops with remaining ¹/₄ cup granulated sugar.

3 Bake 7 to 9 minutes or until cookies are firm but not brown. Cool on cookie sheets 1 minute. Remove to wire racks; cool completely.

4 For filling, beat 1¹/₄ cups butter and powdered sugar in large bowl with electric mixer at low speed until combined. Add 3 tablespoons cream, 1 teaspoon vanilla and pinch of salt; beat until well blended. Increase speed to medium-high; beat 5 minutes or until very fluffy, adding additional cream if filling is too stiff. Divide among five or six bowls; tint with food coloring.

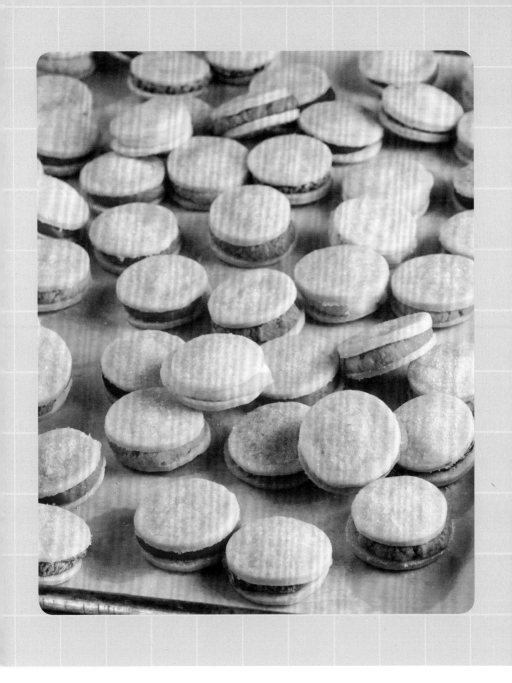

5 Place each color of filling in piping bag or small plastic food storage bag with $1/2$ inch cut from one corner. Squeeze about 2 teaspoons filling onto flat side of one cookie; top with another cookie. Repeat with remaining cookies and filling. Store cookies in airtight container in refrigerator.

Dark Chocolate Dreams

makes 14 cookies

- ¹/₂ cup all-purpose flour
- ³/₄ teaspoon espresso powder *or* ¹/₄ teaspoon ground cinnamon
- ¹/₂ teaspoon baking powder
- ¹/₄ teaspoon salt
- 16 ounces bittersweet chocolate, coarsely chopped
- ¹/₄ cup (¹/₂ stick) butter
- 1¹/₂ cups sugar
- 3 eggs
- 1 teaspoon vanilla
- 1 package (12 ounces) white chocolate chips
- 1 cup dark chocolate chips or chopped pecans

1 Preheat oven to 350°F. Grease cookie sheets or line with parchment paper. Whisk flour, espresso powder, baking powder and salt in small bowl.

2 Melt chocolate and butter in medium saucepan over low heat, stirring constantly until smooth. Cool slightly.

3 Beat sugar, eggs and vanilla with electric mixer at medium-high speed about 6 minutes or until very thick and mixture turns pale color. Reduce speed to low; gradually beat in chocolate mixture until well blended. Gradually beat in flour mixture until blended. Fold in white and dark chocolate chips.

4 Drop dough by level ¹/₃ cupfuls 3 inches apart onto prepared cookie sheets. Flatten into 4-inch circles with moistened fingers.

5 Bake 12 minutes or just until firm and surface begins to crack. *Do not overbake.* Cool on cookie sheets 5 minutes. Remove to wire racks; cool completely.

Pumpkin White Chocolate Drops

makes about 3 dozen cookies

2 cups all-purpose flour

1 teaspoon pumpkin pie spice

½ teaspoon salt

½ teaspoon baking powder

¼ teaspoon baking soda

1 cup granulated sugar

1 cup (2 sticks) butter, softened

½ (15-ounce) can pumpkin purée

1 egg

1 cup white chocolate chips

1 cup prepared cream cheese frosting

1 Preheat oven to 375°F. Line cookie sheets with parchment paper or spray with nonstick cooking spray. Whisk flour, pumpkin pie spice, salt, baking powder and baking soda in medium bowl.

2 Beat granulated sugar and butter in large bowl with electric mixer at medium speed about 3 minutes or until light and fluffy. Add pumpkin and egg; beat until well blended. Add flour mixture; beat at low speed just until blended. Stir in white chocolate chips. Drop dough by tablespoonfuls about 2 inches apart onto prepared cookie sheets.

3 Bake 12 to 15 minutes or until set and lightly browned. Cool on cookie sheets 1 minute. Remove to wire racks; cool completely.

4 Spread frosting over cookies. Store leftovers in airtight container in refrigerator.

Brownie Hearts
makes about 2 dozen hearts

³/₄ cup (1¹/₂ sticks) butter

4 ounces unsweetened chocolate, chopped

1³/₄ cups sugar

4 eggs

1 teaspoon vanilla

¹/₂ teaspoon salt

1 cup all-purpose flour

1 container (16 ounces) white frosting

Pink or red food coloring

Assorted pink, red and white decors

1 Preheat oven to 350°F. Line 13×9-inch baking pan with parchment paper, leaving overhang on two long sides.

2 Melt butter and chocolate in medium saucepan over very low heat until smooth, stirring frequently. Remove from heat.

3 Gradually stir in sugar until well blended. Add eggs one at a time, mixing well after each addition. Stir in vanilla and salt. Stir in flour until blended. Spread batter evenly in prepared pan.

4 Bake about 23 minutes or until toothpick inserted into center comes out with fudgy crumbs. Cool completely in pan on wire rack. Remove from pan using parchment.

5 Place frosting in medium bowl; tint with food coloring. Cut out hearts from brownies with 2- to 3-inch cookie cutter. Spread frosting over each heart; decorate with decors as desired.

Make a Message Cookies

makes about 3 dozen cookies

COOKIES

1½ cups all-purpose flour

1 teaspoon ground cinnamon

½ teaspoon baking soda

½ teaspoon salt

½ teaspoon ground ginger

¼ teaspoon baking powder

½ cup (1 stick) butter, softened

⅓ cup packed brown sugar

¼ cup molasses

1 egg white

½ teaspoon vanilla

LEMONADE ROYAL ICING

3¾ cups powdered sugar

6 tablespoons thawed frozen lemonade concentrate

3 tablespoons meringue powder

Food coloring, colored sugars, sprinkles and assorted small candies

1 Whisk flour, cinnamon, baking soda, salt, ginger and baking powder in small bowl. Beat butter, brown sugar, molasses, egg white and vanilla in large bowl with electric mixer at high speed until smooth. Gradually beat in flour mixture at low speed just until blended. Wrap dough in plastic wrap; refrigerate 1 hour or until firm.

2 Preheat oven to 350°F. Line cookie sheets with parchment paper.

3 Divide dough into four pieces. Working with one piece at a time, roll out dough on floured surface to ⅛-inch thickness. Cut out letter shapes using 2½-inch cookie cutters. Place cutouts on prepared cookie sheets. Repeat with remaining dough.

4 Bake 6 to 8 minutes or until edges begin to brown. Remove cookies to wire racks; cool completely.

5 For icing, beat powdered sugar, lemonade concentrate and meringue powder in large bowl with electric mixer at high speed until smooth.

6 Tint icing desired colors with food coloring. Spread or pipe icing onto cookies; decorate with colored sugars, sprinkles and assorted small candies.

Chocolate Raspberry Bars

makes 16 bars

1⅓ cups all-purpose flour

1 cup quick or old-fashioned oats

⅓ cup unsweetened cocoa powder

1 teaspoon baking powder

½ teaspoon salt

¼ teaspoon baking soda

1 cup packed brown sugar

½ cup (1 stick) butter, softened

2 eggs

1 cup mini candy-coated chocolate pieces

⅓ cup seedless raspberry jam

1 Preheat oven to 350°F. Grease 9-inch square baking pan.

2 Combine flour, oats, cocoa, baking powder, salt and baking soda in medium bowl. Beat brown sugar and butter in large bowl with electric mixer at medium speed until smooth and creamy. Beat in eggs until well blended. Add flour mixture; beat until blended. Stir in chocolate candies.

3 Reserve 1 cup dough; spread remaining dough in prepared pan. Spread preserves evenly over dough to within ½ inch of edges of pan. Drop teaspoonfuls of reserved dough over preserves.

4 Bake 25 to 30 minutes or until bars are slightly firm near edges. Cool completely on wire rack Cut into bars.

44

Chocolate Caramel Thumbprint Cookies

makes 2½ dozen cookies

COOKIES

1½ cups all-purpose flour

¾ cup unsweetened cocoa powder

½ teaspoon salt

1 cup (2 sticks) butter, softened

⅔ cup packed brown sugar

2 eggs, separated

1 teaspoon vanilla

2 cups finely chopped pecans

CARAMEL FILLING

½ cup packed brown sugar

¼ cup (½ stick) butter

2 tablespoons whipping cream

Pinch of salt

2 tablespoons powdered sugar

1 Preheat oven to 375°F. Line cookie sheets with parchment paper or leave ungreased. Whisk flour, cocoa and ½ teaspoon salt in small bowl.

2 Beat butter and ⅔ cup brown sugar in large bowl with electric mixer at medium speed until light and fluffy. Beat in egg yolks and vanilla until well blended. Gradually beat in flour mixture at low speed just until blended. Shape level tablespoonfuls of dough into balls.

3 Whisk egg whites in small bowl. Place pecans in medium bowl. Dip balls one at a time into egg whites, turning to coat completely and letting excess drip back into bowl. Roll in pecans to coat. Place on prepared cookie sheets. Press thumb firmly into center of each cookie.

4 Bake about 10 minutes until cookies are set. Quickly repress thumbprints with end of wooden spoon. Cool on cookie sheets 5 minutes. Remove to wire rack; cool completely.

5 For filling, combine ½ cup brown sugar and ¼ cup butter in small saucepan. Cook over medium heat until mixture begins to boil, stirring constantly; boil 1 minute, stirring constantly. Remove from heat; stir in cream and pinch of salt. Cool 15 minutes. Whisk in powdered sugar until smooth. Fill each cookie with about ½ teaspoon filling.

Rocky Road Brownies

makes 12 to 16 brownies

1 package (about 18 ounces) dark or double chocolate brownie mix, plus ingredients to prepare mix

2 cups mini marshmallows

1/2 cup chopped walnuts

8 ounces semisweet chocolate, chopped *or* 1 1/2 cups semisweet chocolate chips

1 Grease 13×9-inch baking pan or line with parchment paper. Prepare brownie mix according to package directions. Fold in marshmallows and walnuts. Pour batter into prepared pan.

2 Bake brownies according to package directions. Immediately sprinkle chocolate over top of hot brownies. Cool completely in pan on wire rack. Cut into bars.

Giant Chocolate Chip Walnut Cookies

makes 12 large cookies

1³/₄ cups all-purpose flour

1 cup cake flour

1 teaspoon baking powder

³/₄ teaspoon baking soda

³/₄ teaspoon salt

1 cup (2 sticks) cold butter, cut into pieces

³/₄ cup packed brown sugar

¹/₂ cup granulated sugar

2 eggs

1 teaspoon vanilla

2 cups coarsely chopped walnuts

2 cups semisweet chocolate chips

1 Preheat oven to 400°F. Line two cookie sheets with parchment paper. Position oven rack in center of oven.

2 Whisk all-purpose flour, cake flour, baking powder, baking soda and salt in medium bowl. Beat butter, brown sugar and granulated sugar in large bowl with electric mixer at medium speed 2 minutes or until smooth and creamy. Add eggs one at a time, beating until well blended after each addition. Beat in vanilla. Add flour mixture; beat at low speed just until blended. Stir in walnuts and chocolate chips until blended.

3 Shape dough into 12 mounds slightly smaller than a tennis ball (about 4 ounces each); arrange 2 inches apart on prepared baking sheets (six cookies per baking sheet).

4 Bake one sheet at a time about 12 minutes or until tops are light golden brown. (Cover loosely with foil if cookies are browning too quickly.) Place cookie sheet on wire rack; cool 15 minutes. (Cookies will continue to bake while standing.) Serve warm.

50

Apple Walnut Snack Cake

makes 12 servings

3 cups all-purpose flour

1 teaspoon baking soda

1 teaspoon salt

1 teaspoon ground cinnamon

1 cup chopped walnuts

1½ cups granulated sugar

1 cup vegetable oil

2 eggs

2 teaspoons vanilla

2 medium tart apples, peeled and chopped

Powdered sugar (optional)

1 Preheat oven to 325°F. Spray 10-inch tube pan with nonstick cooking spray.

2 Whisk flour, baking soda, salt and cinnamon in large bowl. Stir in walnuts. Combine granulated sugar, oil, eggs and vanilla in medium bowl; mix well. Stir in apples. Add to flour mixture; stir just until blended. Spread batter evenly in prepared pan.

3 Bake 1 hour or until toothpick inserted near center comes out clean. Cool in pan on wire rack 10 minutes. Loosen edges with small spatula, if necessary. Invert onto serving plate; cool completely.

4 Sprinkle with powdered sugar just before serving, if desired.

Confetti Bundt Cake

makes 16 servings

CAKE

- 3 cups all-purpose flour
- 1 teaspoon salt
- 1 teaspoon baking powder
- $\frac{1}{2}$ cup buttermilk
- $\frac{1}{3}$ cup vegetable oil
- 2 teaspoons vanilla
- 2 cups granulated sugar
- 1 cup (2 sticks) butter, softened
- 1 package (8 ounces) cream cheese, softened
- 5 eggs
- $\frac{1}{2}$ cup rainbow sprinkles

CREAM CHEESE GLAZE

- 2 ounces cream cheese, softened
- $\frac{1}{4}$ cup ($\frac{1}{2}$ stick) butter, softened
- 2 cups powdered sugar
- 3 tablespoons milk
- $\frac{1}{4}$ teaspoon vanilla

1 Preheat oven to 325°F. Grease and flour 12-cup (10-inch) bundt pan.

2 Whisk flour, salt and baking powder in medium bowl. Whisk buttermilk, oil and 2 teaspoons vanilla in small bowl until blended.

3 Beat granulated sugar, butter and cream cheese in large bowl with electric mixer at medium speed 5 minutes or until light and fluffy. Add eggs one at a time, beating until blended and scraping down bowl after each addition. Alternately add flour mixture and buttermilk mixture in three additions, beating at low speed just until blended. Stir in sprinkles. Pour batter into prepared pan.

4 Bake 1 hour 10 minutes or until toothpick inserted near center comes out with a few moist crumbs. Cool in pan 15 minutes. Invert onto wire rack; cool completely.

5 For glaze, beat cream cheese and $\frac{1}{4}$ cup butter in large bowl with electric mixer at medium speed until smooth and creamy. Gradually add powdered sugar, beating until blended after each addition. Add milk and $\frac{1}{4}$ teaspoon vanilla; beat until blended. Drizzle glaze over cake. Let stand until set. Store leftovers in refrigerator.

Chocolate Espresso Cake

makes 10 to 12 servings

CAKE

- 2 cups cake flour
- 1½ teaspoons baking soda
- ½ teaspoon salt
- 1 cup granulated sugar
- 1 cup packed brown sugar
- ½ cup (1 stick) butter, softened
- 3 eggs
- 4 ounces unsweetened chocolate, melted
- ¾ cup sour cream
- 1 teaspoon vanilla
- 1 cup brewed espresso*

FROSTING

- ½ cup (1 stick) butter, softened
- 4 cups powdered sugar
- ¼ cup brewed espresso*
- ½ cup semisweet chocolate chips, melted
- 1 teaspoon vanilla
- Pinch of salt

*Or use instant espresso powder or instant coffee prepared according to package directions.

1 Preheat oven to 350°F. Spray two 9-inch round cake pans nonstick cooking spray. Line bottoms with parchment paper; spray paper with nonstick cooking spray. Whisk flour, baking soda and salt in medium bowl.

2 Beat granulated sugar, brown sugar and ½ cup butter in large bowl with electric mixer at medium speed until light and fluffy. Add eggs one at a time, beating well after each addition. Add melted unsweetened chocolate, sour cream and vanilla; beat until blended. Add flour mixture alternately with espresso, mixing at low speed after each addition. Pour batter evenly into prepared pans.

3 Bake about 30 minutes or until toothpick inserted into center comes out clean. Cool in pans on wire rack 10 minutes. Invert onto wire rack; peel off parchment. Cool completely.

4 For frosting, beat ½ cup butter in large bowl with electric mixer at medium speed until creamy. Gradually add powdered sugar and ¼ cup espresso; beat until smooth. Beat in melted semisweet chocolate, 1 teaspoon vanilla and pinch of salt; beat at medium-high speed until very light and fluffy.

5 Place one cake layer on serving plate. Spread with 1½ cups frosting. Top with remaining cake layer; spread remaining frosting over top and side of cake.

Touchdown Treats

makes about 24 pops

$^1/_2$ baked and cooled 13×9-inch cake*

$^1/_2$ cup plus 2 tablespoons frosting

1 package (14 to 16 ounces) chocolate candy coating *or* melting discs *or* 16 ounces chocolate almond bark, chopped

24 lollipop sticks

Foam block

White decorator frosting

*Prepare a cake from a mix according to package directions or use your favorite recipe (try the Devil's Food Party Cake on page 64). Cake must be cooled completely.

1 Line large baking sheet with waxed paper. Use hands to crumble cake into large bowl. (You should end up with fine crumbs and no large cake pieces remaining.)

2 Add frosting to cake crumbs; mix with hands until well blended. Shape mixture into tapered oval football shapes (about 2 tablespoons cake mixture each); place on prepared baking sheet. Cover with plastic wrap; refrigerate at least 1 hour or freeze 10 minutes to firm.

3 When cake balls are firm, place candy coating in deep microwavable bowl. Melt according to package directions. Dip one lollipop stick about $^1/_2$ inch into melted coating; insert stick into cake ball (no more than halfway through). Return cake pop to baking sheet in refrigerator to set. Repeat with remaining cake balls and sticks.

4 Working with one cake pop at a time, hold stick and dip cake ball into melted coating to cover completely, letting excess coating drip off. Rotate stick gently and/or tap stick on edge of bowl, if necessary, to remove excess coating. Place cake pop in foam block.

5 Pipe laces on cake pops with white frosting.

Pineapple Upside Down Cake

makes 10 servings

TOPPING

1 small pineapple*

¹/₄ cup (¹/₂ stick) butter

¹/₂ cup packed brown sugar

Stemmed maraschino cherries

CAKE

2 cups all-purpose flour

2 teaspoons baking powder

¹/₂ teaspoon baking soda

¹/₂ teaspoon salt

¹/₂ cup (1 stick) butter, softened

1 cup granulated sugar

1 egg

1 teaspoon vanilla

1 cup buttermilk

*Or use canned pineapple rings and skip step 2. Proceed with step 3.

1 Preheat oven to 350°F. Spray 9-inch round cake pan with nonstick cooking spray.

2 Remove top and bottom of pineapple. Cut off outside of pineapple and remove eyes. Cut pineapple crosswise into ¹/₄-inch slices. Remove core with ¹/₂-inch cookie cutter or sharp knife.

3 For topping, cook and stir ¹/₄ cup butter and brown sugar in medium skillet over medium heat until melted and smooth. Remove from heat. Pour into prepared pan. Arrange pineapple slices in pan, placing cherries in centers of pineapple and between slices. Reserve remaining pineapple for another use.

4 Whisk flour, baking powder, baking soda and salt in medium bowl. Beat ¹/₂ cup butter and granulated sugar in large bowl with electric mixer at medium speed until well blended. Beat in egg and vanilla. Add flour mixture alternately with buttermilk, mixing at low speed just until blended after each addition. Pour batter over pineapple.

5 Bake about 1 hour or until toothpick inserted into center comes out clean. Cool in pan on wire rack 10 minutes. Run thin knife around edge of pan to loosen cake. Invert onto serving plate; cool completely.

Red Velvet Cake
makes 10 to 12 servings

CAKE

- 2 cups all-purpose flour
- 2 tablespoons unsweetened cocoa powder
- 1 teaspoon salt
- 1¼ cups buttermilk
- 1 bottle (1 ounce) red food coloring
- 1 teaspoon vanilla
- 1½ cups granulated sugar
- 1 cup (2 sticks) butter, softened
- 2 eggs
- 1 tablespoon white or cider vinegar
- 1½ teaspoons baking soda

FROSTING

- 2 packages (8 ounces each) cream cheese, softened
- ½ cup (1 stick) butter, softened
- 6 cups powdered sugar
- ¼ cup milk
- 2 teaspoons vanilla
- 4 ounces white chocolate, shaved with vegetable peeler

1 Preheat oven to 350°F. Spray three 9-inch cake pans with nonstick cooking spray. Line bottoms of pans with parchment paper; spray paper with cooking spray.

2 Whisk flour, cocoa and salt in medium bowl. Combine buttermilk, food coloring and vanilla in small bowl.

3 Beat granulated sugar and 1 cup butter in large bowl with electric mixer at medium speed 5 minutes or until light and fluffy. Add eggs one at a time, beating until well blended after each addition. Add flour mixture alternately with buttermilk mixture, beating at low speed after each addition. Stir vinegar into baking soda in small bowl. Add to batter; stir gently until blended. Pour batter into prepared pans.

4 Bake about 20 minutes or until toothpick inserted into centers comes out clean. Cool in pans 10 minutes. Invert onto wire racks; peel off parchment. Cool completely.

5 For frosting, beat cream cheese and ½ cup butter in large bowl with electric mixer at medium speed until creamy. Add powdered sugar, milk and 2 teaspoons vanilla; beat at low speed until blended. Beat at medium speed until smooth.

6 Place one cake layer on serving plate; spread with 1$\frac{1}{2}$ cups frosting. Top with second cake layer; spread with 1$\frac{1}{2}$ cups frosting. Top with remaining cake layer; spread remaining frosting over top and side of cake. Press white chocolate shavings onto side of cake.

Devil's Food Party Cake

makes 12 to 16 servings

CAKE

1½ cups granulated sugar

1½ cups all-purpose flour

¾ cup unsweetened cocoa powder

½ cup packed brown sugar

1½ teaspoons baking soda

1½ teaspoons baking powder

1 teaspoon salt

1 cup buttermilk or milk

2 eggs

½ cup vegetable oil

1 teaspoon vanilla

2 teaspoons instant coffee granules or instant espresso powder

1 cup boiling water

FROSTING

1 package (12 ounces) dark chocolate chips

¼ teaspoon salt

1 cup whipping cream

2 cups powdered sugar

Colored decors (optional)

1 Preheat oven to 350°F. Spray 13×9-inch baking pan with nonstick cooking spray or line with parchment paper.

2 For cake, combine granulated sugar, flour, cocoa, brown sugar, baking soda, baking powder and 1 teaspoon salt in large bowl of electric mixer; mix at low speed until blended. Add buttermilk, eggs, oil and 1 teaspoon vanilla; beat at medium speed 2 minutes.

3 Stir coffee granules into boiling water in measuring cup or small bowl until well blended. Stir into batter. (Batter will be thin.) Pour batter into prepared pan.

4 Bake about 30 minutes or until top appears dry and toothpick inserted into center comes out clean. Cool completely in pan on wire rack.

5 For frosting, place chocolate chips and ¼ teaspoon salt in large bowl. Bring cream to a simmer in small saucepan over medium heat. Pour cream over chips; swirl to coat. Let stand 5 minutes; whisk until smooth. Cool to room temperature. Add powdered sugar; beat with electric mixer at low speed until blended. Increase speed to medium-high; beat 1 to 2 minutes or until frosting is fluffy and smooth.

6 Spread frosting over cake; sprinkle with decors, if desired.

Cinnamon Swirl Coffeecake

makes 9 to 12 servings

FILLING AND TOPPING

- 1/3 cup all-purpose flour
- 1/3 cup granulated sugar
- 1/3 cup packed brown sugar
- 1 1/2 tablespoons ground cinnamon
- 1/4 teaspoon salt
- 1/8 teaspoon ground allspice
- 3 tablespoons melted butter

CAKE

- 2 cups all-purpose flour
- 1 1/2 teaspoons baking powder
- 3/4 teaspoon baking soda
- 1/2 teaspoon salt
- 9 tablespoons butter, softened
- 1 1/4 cups granulated sugar
- 3 eggs
- 1/2 cup sour cream
- 2 teaspoons vanilla
- 3/4 cup milk

1 Preheat oven to 350°F. Spray 9-inch square baking pan with nonstick cooking spray.

2 For filling, combine 1/3 cup flour, 1/3 cup granulated sugar, brown sugar, cinnamon, 1/4 teaspoon salt and allspice in small bowl; mix well. For topping, remove half of mixture to another small bowl; stir in melted butter until blended.

3 For cake, combine 2 cups flour, baking powder, baking soda and 1/2 teaspoon salt in medium bowl; mix well. Combine 9 tablespoons butter and 1 1/4 cups granulated sugar in large bowl; beat with electric mixer at medium speed 3 minutes or until light and fluffy. Add eggs, sour cream and vanilla; beat until well blended. Add flour mixture alternately with milk in two additions, beating at low speed until blended. Spread half of batter in prepared pan; sprinkle evenly with filling. Spread remaining batter over filling with dampened hands. Sprinkle with topping.

4 Bake 45 to 50 minutes or until toothpick inserted into center comes out clean. Cool completely in pan on wire rack.

Strawberry Cream Shortcake
makes 6 servings

CAKE

1½ cups all-purpose flour

2 teaspoons baking powder

½ teaspoon salt

½ cup (1 stick) butter, softened

1 cup granulated sugar

1 teaspoon vanilla

2 eggs

½ cup plus 2 tablespoons buttermilk

FROSTING

1 package (8 ounces) cream cheese, softened

¾ cup powdered sugar

Pinch of salt

1¼ cups whipping cream

1 teaspoon vanilla (optional)

1 cup strawberry fruit spread*

STRAWBERRIES

1 package (16 ounces) fresh strawberries, stemmed and cut into wedges

½ cup granulated sugar

*Or purée 1 cup strawberry jam or preserves in food processor or blender until smooth.

1 Preheat oven to 350°F. Grease and flour three 8-inch square baking pans. Line bottoms of pans with parchment paper; spray paper with nonstick cooking spray. Whisk flour, baking powder and ½ teaspoon salt in small bowl.

2 Beat butter and 1 cup granulated sugar in large bowl with electric mixer at medium speed 3 to 5 minutes or until light and fluffy. Beat in vanilla. Add eggs one at a time, beating well after each addition. Add flour mixture alternately with buttermilk, mixing at low speed just until blended after each addition. Scrape side of bowl; beat 30 seconds or until well blended. Divide batter evenly among prepared pans; spread evenly to completely cover bottoms of pans. (Layers will be very thin.)

3 Bake 16 to 18 minutes or until edges are very lightly browned and toothpick inserted into centers comes out clean. Cool in pans on wire rack 10 minutes. Remove from pans; cool completely on parchment paper on wire rack.

4 For frosting, whip cream cheese, powdered sugar and pinch of salt in large bowl with electric mixer fitted with whisk attachment at low speed 1 minute or until blended. Increase speed to medium; whip 3 to 5 minutes or until light and fluffy. Scrape side of bowl and whip 1 minute. With mixer running at medium speed, very slowly drizzle in cream; whip until frosting is fluffy and holds stiff peaks. Stir in 1 teaspoon vanilla, if desired.

5 Peel off parchment from cake layers. Place one layer, top side down, on serving plate or cutting board. Top with $^1/_2$ cup fruit spread, spreading to within $^1/_2$ inch of edge. Spread $^3/_4$ cup frosting over fruit spread. Top with second cake layer, top side down; repeat layers of fruit spread and frosting. Top with remaining cake layer, top side up; spread with remaining frosting. Refrigerate at least 2 hours before serving. Meanwhile, combine strawberries and $^1/_2$ cup granulated sugar in medium bowl; cover and refrigerate until ready to serve.

6 To serve, trim about $^1/_2$ inch from each side of cake. Cut cake into six pieces; place on serving plates. Spoon strawberry mixture over and around cake.

Maple Pumpkin Cake

makes 10 to 12 servings

CAKE

2³/₄ cups all-purpose flour

1 tablespoon baking powder

1¹/₂ teaspoons baking soda

1¹/₂ teaspoons ground cinnamon

¹/₂ teaspoon salt

¹/₄ teaspoon ground allspice

¹/₄ teaspoon ground nutmeg

¹/₈ teaspoon ground ginger

1¹/₂ cups granulated sugar

³/₄ cup (1¹/₂ sticks) butter

3 eggs

1¹/₂ cups canned pumpkin

1 cup buttermilk

FROSTING

1 cup (2 sticks) butter, softened

4 cups powdered sugar

1 teaspoon vanilla

¹/₂ teaspoon maple flavoring

1 Preheat oven to 350°F. Grease and flour two (9-inch) round cake pans. Whisk flour, baking powder, baking soda, cinnamon, salt, allspice, nutmeg and ginger in medium bowl.

2 Beat granulated sugar and butter in large bowl with electric mixer at medium speed until light and fluffy. Add eggs one at a time, beating well after each addition. Combine pumpkin and buttermilk in medium bowl.

3 Add flour mixture alternately with pumpkin mixture, mixing at low speed just until blended after each addition. Pour batter into prepared pans.

4 Bake 40 to 45 minutes or until toothpick inserted into centers comes out clean. Cool in pans 10 minutes. Remove to wire racks; cool completely.

5 For frosting, beat 1 cup butter in large bowl with electric mixer at medium speed until creamy. Gradually add powdered sugar; add vanilla and maple flavoring. Beat at medium-high speed until light and fluffy.

6 Place one cake layer on serving plate. Top with about 1 cup frosting; top with remaining cake layer. Spread remaining frosting over top and side of cake.

Almond Flour Pound Cake

makes 10 to 12 servings

2 cups almond flour

1 teaspoon baking powder

½ teaspoon salt

¼ teaspoon ground ginger

¼ teaspoon ground cardamom

½ cup (1 stick) butter, softened

4 ounces cream cheese, softened

¾ cup granulated sugar

2 tablespoons brown sugar

4 eggs

1 teaspoon vanilla

1 tablespoon sliced almonds

1 Preheat oven to 350°F. Spray 9×5-inch loaf pan (or two mini loaf pans) with nonstick cooking spray. Whisk almond flour, baking powder, salt, ginger and cardamom in medium bowl.

2 Beat butter, cream cheese, granulated sugar and brown sugar in large bowl with electric mixer at medium speed until well blended. Add eggs one at a time, beating well after each addition. Beat in vanilla. Gradually add almond flour mixture, beating at low speed until blended. Pour batter into prepared pan; sprinkle with sliced almonds.

3 Bake 45 to 55 minutes or until toothpick inserted into center comes out clean. Cool in pan 10 minutes. Remove to wire rack; cool completely.

Peppermint Ribbon Cake

makes 16 servings

1 package (about 15 ounces) yellow or white cake mix *without* pudding in the mix

1 package (4-serving size) vanilla instant pudding and pie filling mix

1 cup sour cream

4 eggs

$1/2$ cup vegetable oil

$1/3$ cup water

$3/4$ teaspoon peppermint extract

Red food coloring

1 cup mini chocolate chips

2 cups powdered sugar

2 to 3 tablespoons milk

$1/2$ cup crushed peppermint candies (about 12 round candies)

1 Preheat oven to 350°F. Grease and flour 10- or 12-cup bundt pan.

2 Beat cake mix, pudding mix, sour cream, eggs, oil and water in large bowl with electric mixer at low speed 1 minute or until blended. Beat at medium speed 2 minutes or until smooth.

3 Combine $1^1/2$ cups batter, peppermint extract and 16 drops of red food coloring in small bowl; mix well. Stir chocolate chips into remaining batter. Spread half of chocolate chip batter in prepared pan. Spoon peppermint batter on top. Spread remaining chocolate chip batter over peppermint batter.

4 Bake 50 to 60 minutes or until toothpick inserted near center comes out clean. Cool in pan 20 minutes. Invert onto serving plate; cool completely.

5 Whisk powdered sugar and 2 tablespoons milk in small bowl until smooth. Add remaining 1 tablespoon milk, if necessary, to reach drizzling consistency. Drizzle glaze over cake. Sprinkle with crushed candies.

Chocolate-Orange Lava Cakes

makes 4 servings

½ cup semisweet
chocolate chips

¼ cup (½ stick) butter

½ cup powdered
sugar, plus
additional for
garnish

2 eggs

2 egg yolks

1 teaspoon grated
orange peel

3 tablespoons all-
purpose flour

⅛ teaspoon salt

Orange peel strips
(optional)

1 Preheat oven to 425°F. Spray four
4-ounce ramekins with nonstick
cooking spray; place on baking sheet.

2 Combine chocolate chips and butter in
medium microwavable bowl. Microwave
on HIGH 45 seconds; stir until melted
and smooth. Add ½ cup powdered
sugar; stir until blended. Add eggs, egg
yolks and orange peel; whisk until well
blended. Add flour and salt; stir until
smooth. Divide batter evenly among
prepared ramekins.

3 Bake about 10 minutes or until edges
are set but centers are still soft. Let
stand 1 minute. Invert cakes onto plates,
waiting 10 seconds before removing
ramekins. Invert cakes again to serve
top side up. Sprinkle with additional
powdered sugar; garnish with orange
peel strips. Serve warm.

Blueberry Muffins

makes 12 muffins

2 cups all-purpose flour

2¹⁄₄ teaspoons baking powder

¹⁄₂ teaspoon salt

¹⁄₄ teaspoon baking soda

1 cup granulated sugar

¹⁄₂ cup (1 stick) butter, melted

³⁄₄ cup buttermilk

2 eggs

1 teaspoon grated lemon peel

1¹⁄₂ cups blueberries

2 tablespoons sparkling sugar *or* 4 tablespoons turbinado sugar

1 Preheat oven to 375°F. Line 12 standard (2¹⁄₂-inch) muffin cups with paper baking cups or spray with nonstick cooking spray.

2 Whisk flour, baking powder, salt and baking soda in medium bowl. Whisk granulated sugar and butter in large bowl until well blended. Add buttermilk, eggs and lemon peel; whisk until well blended. Add flour mixture; stir just until moistened. Fold in blueberries.

3 Spoon batter evenly into prepared muffin cups, filling almost full. Sprinkle ¹⁄₂ teaspoon sparkling sugar or 1 teaspoon turbinado sugar over each muffin.

4 Bake 20 to 22 minutes or until toothpick inserted into centers comes out clean. Cool in pan 10 minutes. Remove to wire rack; serve warm or cool completely.

Piña Colada Muffins

makes 18 muffins

2 cups all-purpose flour

³/₄ cup sugar

¹/₂ cup flaked coconut

2 teaspoons baking powder

¹/₂ teaspoon baking soda

¹/₂ teaspoon salt

2 eggs

1 cup sour cream

1 can (8 ounces) crushed pineapple in juice, undrained

¹/₄ cup (¹/₂ stick) butter, melted

¹/₈ teaspoon coconut extract

Additional flaked coconut (optional)

1 Preheat oven to 400°F. Line 18 standard (2¹/₂-inch) muffin cups with paper baking cups or spray with nonstick cooking spray.

2 Whisk flour, sugar, ¹/₂ cup coconut, baking powder, baking soda and salt in large bowl.

3 Whisk eggs in medium bowl until frothy. Add sour cream, pineapple with juice, butter and coconut extract; whisk until well blended. Add to flour mixture; stir just until moistened. Spoon batter evenly into prepared muffin cups, filling three-fourths full.

4 Bake 15 to 18 minutes or until toothpick inserted into centers comes out clean. If desired, sprinkle tops of muffins with additional coconut after first 10 minutes. Cool in pans 2 minutes. Remove to wire racks; cool completely.

Cream Scones
makes 8 servings

2¼ cups all-purpose
    flour

¼ cup granulated
    sugar

1 tablespoon baking
    powder

½ teaspoon salt

6 tablespoons cold
    butter, cut into
    pieces

⅔ cup whipping cream

2 eggs

Coarse white
    decorating sugar

1 Preheat oven to 425°F. Line baking sheet with parchment paper.

2 Whisk flour, granulated sugar, baking powder and salt in large bowl. Cut in butter with pastry blender or fingertips until coarse crumbs form.

3 Whisk cream and eggs in small bowl; reserve 1 tablespoon egg mixture. Pour remaining egg mixture over flour mixture; stir just until dough forms.

4 Turn out dough onto lightly floured surface. Shape into a ball; pat into 8-inch disc. Cut into eight wedges; place 2 inches apart on prepared baking sheet. Brush reserved egg mixture over tops; sprinkle with coarse sugar.

5 Bake 12 to 14 minutes or until golden brown and toothpick inserted into center comes out clean. Remove to wire rack; serve warm or cool completely.

CHOCOLATE LAVENDER SCONES: Add 1 teaspoon dried lavender to dry ingredients. Stir ½ cup coarsely chopped semisweet chocolate into dough before shaping.

GINGER PEACH SCONES: Stir ⅓ cup chopped dried peaches and 1 tablespoon finely chopped crystallized ginger into dough before shaping.

LEMON POPPY SEED SCONES: Stir grated peel of 1 lemon (about 4 teaspoons) and 1 tablespoon poppy seeds into dough before shaping. Omit coarse sugar topping. Combine 1 cup powdered sugar and 2 tablespoons lemon juice in small bowl. Drizzle over slightly cooled scones.

MAPLE PECAN SCONES: Stir $1/2$ cup coarsely chopped pecans into dough before shaping. Omit coarse sugar topping. Combine $3/4$ cup powdered sugar and 2 tablespoons maple syrup in small bowl. Drizzle over slightly cooled scones.

White Chocolate Chunk Muffins

makes 12 jumbo muffins

2½ cups all-purpose flour

1 cup packed brown sugar

⅓ cup unsweetened cocoa powder

2 teaspoons baking soda

½ teaspoon salt

1⅓ cups buttermilk

¼ cup (½ stick) plus 2 tablespoons butter, melted

2 eggs

1½ teaspoons vanilla

1½ cups chopped white chocolate

1 Preheat oven to 400°F. Grease 12 jumbo (3½-inch) muffin cups or line with paper baking cups.

2 Whisk flour, brown sugar, cocoa, baking soda and salt in large bowl. Whisk buttermilk, butter, eggs and vanilla in medium bowl until blended. Stir into flour mixture just until moistened. Fold in white chocolate. Spoon evenly into prepared muffin cups, filling about half full.

3 Bake 25 to 30 minutes or until toothpick inserted into centers comes out clean. Cool in pan 5 minutes. Remove to wire rack; cool 10 minutes. Serve warm or cool completely.

Honey Scones with Cherry Compote

makes 8 scones

Cherry Compote
(recipe follows)

2 cups all-purpose
flour

1/2 cup old-fashioned
oats

2 tablespoons packed
brown sugar

1 tablespoon
granulated sugar

1 tablespoon baking
powder

1/2 teaspoon salt

6 tablespoons cold
butter, cut into
pieces

1/2 cup whipping cream

1 egg

3 tablespoons honey

1 Prepare Cherry Compote.

2 Preheat oven to 425°F. Line baking
sheet with parchment paper.

3 Whisk flour, oats, brown sugar,
granulated sugar, baking powder and
salt in large bowl. Cut in butter with
pastry blender or fingertips until coarse
crumbs form. Whisk cream, egg and
honey in medium bowl. Add to flour
mixture; stir just until dough forms.

4 Turn out dough onto lightly floured
surface. Pat into 8-inch disc. Cut into
eight wedges; place 2 inches apart on
prepared baking sheet.

5 Bake 12 to 15 minutes or until golden
brown. Cool on wire rack 15 minutes.
Serve warm with Cherry Compote.

Cherry Compote

makes about 2 cups

1 pound fresh Bing
cherries, pitted
and halved

1/4 cup sugar

1/4 cup water

2 tablespoons lemon
juice

1 Combine cherries, sugar, water and
lemon juice in medium saucepan.
Cook over medium heat until sugar
is dissolved and liquid is boiling. Boil
2 minutes. Remove cherries with slotted
spoon; set aside.

2 Reduce heat to medium-low; simmer
liquid 2 to 4 minutes or until thickened.

3 Return cherries to saucepan; remove
from heat. Cool 1 hour before serving.

Apple Butter Spice Muffins
makes 12 muffins

¹/₂ cup sugar

1 teaspoon ground cinnamon

¹/₄ teaspoon ground nutmeg

¹/₈ teaspoon ground allspice

¹/₂ cup chopped pecans or walnuts

2 cups all-purpose flour

2 teaspoons baking powder

¹/₄ teaspoon salt

1 cup milk

¹/₄ cup vegetable oil

1 egg

¹/₄ cup apple butter

1 Preheat oven to 400°F. Line 12 standard (2¹/₂-inch) muffin cups with paper baking cups or spray with nonstick cooking spray.

2 Combine sugar, cinnamon, nutmeg and allspice in large bowl. Remove 2 tablespoons sugar mixture to small bowl; add pecans and toss until coated. Add flour, baking powder and salt to remaining sugar mixture; mix well.

3 Whisk milk, oil and egg in medium bowl until well blended. Add to flour mixture; stir just until dry ingredients are moistened. Spoon 1 tablespoon batter into each prepared muffin cup. Top with 1 teaspoon apple butter; spoon remaining batter evenly over apple butter. Sprinkle with pecan mixture.

4 Bake 18 to 20 minutes or until golden brown and toothpick inserted into centers comes out clean. Cool in pan 5 minutes. Remove to wire rack; cool 10 minutes. Serve warm or cool completely.

Lemon-Cardamom Scones

makes 8 servings

2 cups all-purpose flour

2 tablespoons granulated sugar

2 teaspoons grated lemon peel, divided

2 teaspoons baking powder

³/₄ teaspoon ground cardamom

¹/₂ teaspoon salt

¹/₄ teaspoon baking soda

6 tablespoons cold butter, cut into pieces

²/₃ cup sour cream or whipping cream

1 egg

3 tablespoons powdered sugar

2 teaspoons lemon juice

1 Preheat oven to 400°F. Line baking sheet with parchment paper.

2 Whisk flour, granulated sugar, 1¹/₂ teaspoons lemon peel, baking powder, cardamom, salt and baking soda in large bowl. Cut in butter with pastry blender or fingertips until coarse crumbs form. Whisk sour cream and egg in small bowl until blended. Add to flour mixture; stir just until dough forms.

3 Turn out dough onto lightly floured surface. Knead 10 to 12 times. Pat dough into 8 inch disc; cut into 8 wedges. Place 2 inches apart on prepared baking sheet.

4 Bake 11 to 13 minutes or until golden brown. Cool on baking sheet 10 minutes. Remove to wire rack.

5 Combine powdered sugar, lemon juice and remaining ¹/₂ teaspoon lemon peel in small bowl until smooth; drizzle over warm scones.

LEMON-GINGER SCONES: Substitute ground ginger for ground cardamom.

Lemon Poppy Seed Muffins
makes 18 muffins

2 cups all-purpose flour

1¼ cups granulated sugar

¼ cup poppy seeds

2 tablespoons plus 2 teaspoons grated lemon peel, divided

2 teaspoons baking powder

½ teaspoon baking soda

½ teaspoon ground cardamom

¼ teaspoon salt

2 eggs

½ cup (1 stick) butter, melted

½ cup milk

½ cup plus 2 tablespoons lemon juice, divided

1 cup powdered sugar

1 Preheat oven to 400°F. Line 18 standard (2½-inch) muffin cups with paper baking cups or spray with nonstick cooking spray.

2 Whisk flour, granulated sugar, poppy seeds, 2 tablespoons lemon peel, baking powder, baking soda, cardamom and salt in large bowl. Beat eggs in medium bowl. Add butter, milk and ½ cup lemon juice; beat until well blended. Add to flour mixture; stir just until blended. Spoon batter evenly into prepared muffin cups, filling three-fourths full.

3 Bake 15 to 20 minutes or until toothpick inserted into centers comes out clean. Cool in pans on wire racks 10 minutes.

4 Meanwhile for glaze, combine powdered sugar and remaining 2 teaspoons lemon peel in small bowl; stir in enough remaining lemon juice to make pourable glaze. Place muffins on sheet of parchment paper; drizzle with glaze. Serve warm or cool completely.

Raspberry Streusel Muffins
makes 6 jumbo muffins

STREUSEL TOPPING

1/4 **cup all-purpose flour**

1/4 **cup packed brown sugar**

2 **tablespoons cold butter**

MUFFINS

2 **cups all-purpose flour, divided**

3/4 **cup granulated sugar**

2 **teaspoons baking powder**

1/2 **teaspoon baking soda**

1/2 **teaspoon salt**

1/2 **teaspoon grated lemon peel**

3/4 **cup plus 2 tablespoons milk**

1/3 **cup butter, melted**

1 **egg, beaten**

2 **cups fresh or frozen raspberries (do not thaw)**

1 Preheat oven to 350°F. Spray 6 jumbo (3 1/2-inch) muffin cups with nonstick cooking spray.

2 For topping, combine 1/4 cup flour and brown sugar in small bowl. Cut in 2 tablespoons cold butter with pastry blender or fingertips until mixture forms coarse crumbs.

3 For muffins, reserve 1/4 cup flour in medium bowl. Combine remaining 1 3/4 cups flour, granulated sugar, baking powder, baking soda, salt and lemon peel in large bowl. Whisk milk, melted butter and egg in small bowl until blended. Add to flour mixture; stir just until moistened.

4 Add raspberries to reserved flour; toss gently to coat. Gently fold raspberries into batter. Spoon batter into prepared muffin cups, filling three-fourths full. Sprinkle with topping.

5 Bake 25 to 30 minutes or until toothpick inserted into centers comes out clean. Cool in pan 2 minutes. Remove to wire rack; serve warm or cool completely.

Chocolate Banana Muffins
makes 15 muffins

2 cups all-purpose flour

¼ cup granulated sugar

¼ cup packed brown sugar

1½ teaspoons baking powder

½ teaspoon salt

¼ teaspoon baking soda

1 cup mashed ripe bananas (about 2 large or 3 small)

½ cup (1 stick) butter, melted

2 eggs

⅓ cup buttermilk

1 teaspoon vanilla

1 package (about 11 ounces) semisweet chocolate chips

1 Preheat oven to 375°F. Spray 15 standard (2½-inch) muffin cups with nonstick cooking spray or line with paper baking cups.

2 Whisk flour, granulated sugar, brown sugar, baking powder, salt and baking soda in large bowl. Whisk bananas, butter, eggs, buttermilk and vanilla in medium bowl until well blended. Add to flour mixture; stir just until moistened. Stir in chocolate chips. Spoon batter evenly into prepared muffin cups, filling almost full.

3 Bake 18 to 20 minutes or until toothpick inserted into centers comes out clean. Cool in pans 5 minutes. Remove to wire rack; serve warm or cool completely.

NOTE: If you want to use only one pan, divide the batter evenly among 12 standard muffin cups instead of 15 and fill the cups completely.

BANANA CHOCOLATE CHIP BREAD: Line 9×5-inch loaf pan with parchment paper; spray with nonstick cooking spray. Prepare batter as directed; spread in prepared pan. Bake in preheated 350°F oven about 1 hour 10 minutes or until toothpick inserted into center comes out clean. Cool in pan 10 minutes. Remove to wire rack; serve warm or cool completely.

White Chocolate Cranberry Scones

makes 8 scones

1 cup all-purpose flour

1 cup whole wheat flour

¼ cup plus 2 tablespoons sugar, divided

2 teaspoons baking powder

½ teaspoon salt

½ teaspoon ground nutmeg

6 tablespoons cold butter, cut into pieces

1 cup dried cranberries

1 cup white chocolate chips

2 eggs

⅓ cup plus 1 tablespoon whipping cream, divided

Grated peel of 1 orange

1 Preheat oven to 425°F. Line baking sheet with parchment paper.

2 Whisk flours, ¼ cup sugar, baking powder, salt and nutmeg in medium bowl. Cut in butter with pastry blender or fingertips until coarse crumbs form. Stir in cranberries and white chocolate chips; make well in center of mixture. Beat eggs in small bowl; stir in ⅓ cup cream and orange peel. Pour into center of flour mixture; stir just until dough forms.

3 Turn out dough onto lightly floured surface; knead 8 to 10 times. Shape into 9-inch disc. Place on prepared baking sheet. Score into 8 wedges with sharp knife. Brush with remaining 1 tablespoon cream. Sprinkle evenly with remaining 2 tablespoons sugar.

4 Bake 20 to 23 minutes or until edges are lightly browned and toothpick inserted into center comes out clean. Cool on baking sheet 5 minutes; cut along score lines. Serve warm or cool completely.

Chocolate Peanut Oatmeal Muffins
makes 12 muffins

1 cup buttermilk

1 cup quick or old-fashioned oats

³/₄ cup all-purpose flour

¹/₄ cup unsweetened cocoa powder

1 teaspoon baking powder

³/₄ teaspoon salt

¹/₂ teaspoon baking soda

²/₃ cup packed dark brown sugar

¹/₃ cup vegetable oil

1 egg

1 teaspoon vanilla

³/₄ cup roasted salted peanuts, chopped

1 Preheat oven to 400°F. Line 12 standard (2¹/₂-inch) muffin cups with paper baking cups or spray with nonstick cooking spray.

2 Combine buttermilk and oats in medium bowl; mix well. Let stand 15 minutes.

3 Meanwhile, whisk flour, cocoa, baking powder, salt and baking soda in small bowl. Whisk brown sugar, oil, egg and vanilla in large bowl until well blended. Add oat mixture; mix well. Add flour mixture; stir just until moistend. Stir in peanuts. Spoon batter evenly into prepared muffin cups, filling almost full.

4 Bake 13 to 15 minutes or until toothpick inserted into centers comes out clean. Cool in pan 5 minutes. Remove to wire rack; serve warm or cool completely.

Cheddar Biscuits

makes 15 biscuits

2 cups all-purpose flour

1 tablespoon sugar

1 tablespoon baking powder

2$\frac{1}{4}$ teaspoons garlic powder, divided

$\frac{3}{4}$ teaspoon plus pinch of salt, divided

1 cup whole milk

$\frac{1}{2}$ cup (1 stick) plus 3 tablespoons butter, melted, divided

2 cups (8 ounces) shredded Cheddar cheese

$\frac{1}{2}$ teaspoon dried parsley flakes

1 Preheat oven to 450°F. Line baking sheet with parchment paper.

2 Whisk flour, sugar, baking powder, 2 teaspoons garlic powder and $\frac{3}{4}$ teaspoon salt in large bowl. Add milk and $\frac{1}{2}$ cup butter; stir just until moistened. Gently fold in cheese. Drop scant $\frac{1}{4}$ cupfuls of dough about 1$\frac{1}{2}$ inches apart onto prepared baking sheet.

3 Bake 10 to 12 minutes or until golden brown.

4 Meanwhile, combine remaining 3 tablespoons butter, $\frac{1}{4}$ teaspoon garlic powder, pinch of salt and parsley flakes in small bowl; brush over biscuits immediately after removing from oven. Serve warm.

Glazed Lemon Loaf

makes 8 to 10 servings

BREAD

1½ cups all-purpose flour

½ teaspoon baking powder

½ teaspoon baking soda

½ teaspoon salt

1 cup granulated sugar

3 eggs

½ cup vegetable oil

⅓ cup lemon juice

2 tablespoons butter, melted

1 teaspoon lemon extract

½ teaspoon vanilla

GLAZE

3 tablespoons butter

1½ cups powdered sugar

2 tablespoons lemon juice

1 to 2 teaspoons grated lemon peel

1 Preheat oven to 350°F. Grease and flour 8×4-inch loaf pan.

2 For bread, whisk flour, baking powder, baking soda and salt in large bowl. Whisk granulated sugar, eggs, oil, ⅓ cup lemon juice, 2 tablespoons melted butter, lemon extract and vanilla in medium bowl until well blended. Add to flour mixture; stir just until blended. Pour batter into prepared pan.

3 Bake about 40 minutes or until toothpick inserted into center comes out clean. Cool in pan 10 minutes. Remove to wire rack; cool 10 minutes.

4 Meanwhile for glaze, melt 3 tablespoons butter in small saucepan over medium-low heat. Whisk in powdered sugar, 2 tablespoons lemon juice and 1 teaspoon lemon peel; cook until smooth and hot, whisking constantly. Pour glaze over warm bread; smooth top. Cool completely before slicing. Garnish with additional 1 teaspoon lemon peel, if desired.

Cardamom Rolls

makes 12 rolls

DOUGH

- 1/2 cup water
- 1/2 cup milk
- 1 tablespoon active dry yeast
- 1/2 cup plus 1 teaspoon granulated sugar, divided
- 1/2 cup (1 stick) butter, softened
- 3 eggs
- 1/2 teaspoon vanilla
- 4 cups all-purpose flour, divided
- 3/4 teaspoon salt

FILLING

- 2 tablespoons butter, very soft
- 1/4 cup packed brown sugar
- 1 1/2 teaspoons ground cardamom
- 1 teaspoon ground cinnamon
- 1 tablespoon butter, melted
- Pearl sugar (optional)

1 Heat water and milk in small saucepan to about 115°F. Transfer to small bowl; stir in yeast and 1 teaspoon granulated sugar until dissolved. Let stand 5 minutes or until bubbly.

2 Beat 1/2 cup butter and remaining 1/2 cup granulated sugar in large bowl with electric mixer at medium speed until light and fluffy. Add eggs one at a time, beating well after each addition. Beat in vanilla. Reduce speed to low; beat in yeast mixture, 2 cups flour and salt. Beat at medium speed 2 minutes.

3 Add remaining 2 cups flour; knead with dough hook at low speed until most of flour is incorporated. Beat at medium speed 3 minutes (dough will be sticky). Cover and let rise in warm place about 1 1/2 hours or until doubled in size. Stir down dough. Cover and refrigerate 2 hours or overnight.

4 Roll out dough into 18-inch square on floured surface. Spread 2 tablespoons butter over top half of dough. Sprinkle with brown sugar, cardamom and cinnamon. Fold bottom of dough over filling; pinch ends to seal. Roll into 20×10-inch rectangle. Cut dough crosswise into 12 strips. Cut each strip lengthwise into two or three pieces, leaving them connected at the top. Holding uncut end, wrap cut dough around fingers and pull into knot shape,

turning to expose some of filling. Place on baking sheet. Brush with melted butter; sprinkle with pearl sugar. Let stand 15 minutes.

5 Preheat oven to 375°F. Bake 15 to 20 minutes or until golden brown. Remove to wire rack; serve warm.

Banana Bread à la Mode

makes 6 servings

BREAD

1³/₄ cups all-purpose flour

1 teaspoon baking soda

¹/₂ teaspoon salt

¹/₂ teaspoon ground cinnamon

¹/₄ teaspoon ground nutmeg

2 eggs

3 very ripe bananas, mashed (about 1¹/₂ cups)

1 cup packed brown sugar

¹/₂ cup vegetable oil

¹/₂ cup sour cream

1 teaspoon vanilla

1 cup coarsely chopped walnuts, toasted

SAUCE AND GARNISH

¹/₄ cup (¹/₂ stick) butter

¹/₂ cup packed brown sugar

¹/₂ cup whipping cream

Pinch of salt

1 teaspoon vanilla

2 ripe bananas, sliced

¹/₄ cup sliced almonds

Vanilla ice cream

1 Preheat oven to 350°F. Spray 9×5-inch loaf pan with nonstick cooking spray.

2 Whisk flour, baking soda, ¹/₂ teaspoon salt, cinnamon and nutmeg in large bowl. Beat eggs in medium bowl. Add mashed bananas, 1 cup brown sugar, oil, sour cream and 1 teaspoon vanilla; stir until blended. Add to flour mixture; stir just until moistened. Fold in walnuts. Spread batter in prepared pan.

3 Bake 50 to 55 minutes or until toothpick inserted into center comes out clean. Cool in pan 10 minutes. Remove to wire rack.

4 For sauce, melt butter in small saucepan over medium heat. Add ¹/₂ cup brown sugar; stir until dissolved. Add cream and pinch of salt; bring to a boil, stirring constantly. Remove from heat; stir in 1 teaspoon vanilla.

5 Cut bread into 12 slices; place two slices on each of six serving plates. Pour sauce over banana bread; top with sliced bananas, almonds and ice cream. Drizzle with additional sauce.

Spinach and Feta Stuffed Cheesy Bread

makes about 8 servings

1½ cups (6 ounces) shredded mozzarella or Monterey Jack cheese, divided

4 ounces crumbled feta cheese

¼ cup plus 1 tablespoon grated Parmesan cheese, divided

1 teaspoon minced garlic

1 container (11 ounces) refrigerated French bread dough

1 cup baby spinach

½ cup (2 ounces) shredded Cheddar cheese

¼ teaspoon Italian seasoning or dried parsley flakes

1 Preheat oven to 350°F. Line baking sheet with parchment paper.

2 Combine 1 cup mozzarella, feta, ¼ cup Parmesan and garlic in small bowl; mix well. Unroll dough on prepared baking sheet with long side facing you. Spread half of cheese mixture lengthwise over half of dough; top with spinach and remaining half of cheese mixture. Fold dough in half over filling; press long edge gently to seal.

3 Cut crosswise into 1-inch slices from sealed edge, leaving attached at folded edge (do not separate slices). Top with Cheddar, then remaining ½ cup mozzarella. Sprinkle with Italian seasoning.

4 Bake 25 to 30 minutes or until golden brown. Cut into slices; serve warm.

Cinnamon Buns

makes 12 buns

DOUGH

1 package ($^1/_4$ ounce) active dry yeast

1 cup warm milk (110°F)

2 eggs

$^1/_2$ cup granulated sugar

$^1/_4$ cup ($^1/_2$ stick) butter, softened

1 teaspoon salt

4 to 4$^1/_4$ cups all-purpose flour

FILLING

1 cup packed brown sugar

3 tablespoons ground cinnamon

Pinch of salt

6 tablespoons butter, softened

ICING

1$^1/_2$ cups powdered sugar

3 ounces cream cheese, softened

$^1/_4$ cup ($^1/_2$ stick) butter, softened

$^1/_2$ teaspoon vanilla

$^1/_8$ teaspoon salt

1 Dissolve yeast in warm milk in large bowl of electric mixer. Add eggs, granulated sugar, $^1/_4$ cup butter and 1 teaspoon salt; beat at medium speed until well blended. Add 4 cups flour; beat at low speed until dough begins to come together. Knead with dough hook at low speed 5 minutes or until dough is smooth, elastic and slightly sticky. Add additional flour, 1 tablespoon at a time, if necessary to prevent sticking.

2 Shape dough into a ball. Place in large greased bowl; turn to grease top. Cover and let rise in warm place 1 hour or until doubled in size. Meanwhile for filling, combine brown sugar, cinnamon and pinch of salt in small bowl; mix well.

3 Spray 13×9-inch baking pan with nonstick cooking spray. Roll out dough into 18×14-inch rectangle on floured surface. Spread 6 tablespoons butter evenly over dough; top with cinnamon-sugar mixture. Beginning with long side, tightly roll up dough; pinch seam to seal. Cut log crosswise into 12 slices; place slices cut sides up in prepared pan. Cover and let rise in warm place 30 minutes or until almost doubled in size. Preheat oven to 350°F.

4 Bake 20 to 25 minutes or until golden brown. Meanwhile for icing, combine powdered sugar, cream cheese, $\frac{1}{4}$ cup butter, vanilla and $\frac{1}{8}$ teaspoon salt in medium bowl; beat with electric mixer at medium speed 2 minutes or until smooth and creamy. Spread icing generously over warm cinnamon buns.

Pull-Apart Garlic Cheese Bread

makes 12 servings

3 cups all-purpose flour

1 package (¹/₄ ounce) instant or active dry yeast

1 teaspoon salt

1 cup warm water (120°F)

2 tablespoons olive oil

6 cloves garlic, minced, divided

¹/₄ cup (¹/₂ stick) butter

¹/₄ teaspoon paprika

1 cup grated Parmesan cheese

1 cup (4 ounces) shredded mozzarella cheese

¹/₂ cup pizza sauce

Chopped fresh parsley (optional)

1 Combine flour, yeast and salt in large bowl of electric mixer. Stir in water and oil to form rough dough. Add half of garlic; knead with dough hook at low speed 5 to 7 minutes or until dough is smooth and elastic.

2 Shape dough into a ball. Place in greased bowl; turn to grease top. Cover and let rise in warm place 45 minutes to 1 hour or until doubled in size.

3 Melt butter in small skillet over medium-low heat. Add remaining garlic; cook and stir 1 minute. Stir in paprika; remove from heat. Brush 9-inch springform pan with some of butter mixture. Place 6-ounce ramekin in center of pan. Place Parmesan in shallow bowl.

4 Turn out dough onto lightly floured surface; pat into 9-inch square. Cut into 1-inch squares; roll each square into a ball. Dip half of balls in melted butter mixture; roll in Parmesan to coat. Place around ramekin in prepared pan; sprinkle with ¹/₂ cup mozzarella. Repeat with remaining dough, butter mixture, Parmesan and mozzarella. Cover and let rise in warm place 1 hour or until dough has risen to top of pan.

5 Preheat oven to 350°F. Line baking sheet with foil. Pour pizza sauce into ramekin. Place springform pan on prepared baking sheet.

6 Bake 20 to 25 minutes or until bread is firm and golden brown. Loosen edges of bread with knife; carefully remove side of pan. Sprinkle with parsley, if desired. Serve warm.

Cookie Dough Monkey Bread

makes about 16 servings

1 package (about 16 ounces) break-apart refrigerated chocolate chip cookie dough (24 cookies)

2 packages (7½ ounces each) refrigerated buttermilk biscuits (10 biscuits per package)

1 cup semisweet chocolate chips, divided

¼ cup whipping cream

1 Preheat oven to 350°F. Generously spray 12-cup (10-inch) bundt pan with nonstick cooking spray.

2 Break cookie dough into 24 pieces; split each piece in half to create total of 48 pieces. Separate biscuits; cut each biscuit into four pieces with scissors. Layer half of cookie dough and half of biscuit pieces in prepared pan, alternating doughs. Sprinkle with ¼ cup chocolate chips. Repeat layers with remaining cookie dough and biscuit pieces; sprinkle with ¼ cup chocolate chips.

3 Bake 27 to 30 minutes or until biscuits are golden brown, covering pan loosely with foil during last 10 minutes of baking. Remove pan to wire rack; let stand, covered, 5 minutes. Loosen edges of bread with knife; invert onto serving plate.

4 Pour cream into medium microwavable bowl; microwave on HIGH 1 minute or until simmering. Add remaining ½ cup chocolate chips; stir until chocolate is melted. Let stand 5 minutes to thicken slightly. Drizzle glaze over bread.

Soft Pretzel Bites with Creamy Honey Mustard

makes 12 servings

3/4 cup sour cream

1/4 cup Dijon mustard

3 tablespoons honey

1 package (1/4 ounce) active dry yeast

2 teaspoons sugar

1/2 teaspoon salt

1²/₃ cups warm water (110° to 115°F)

4¹/₂ cups all-purpose flour

2 tablespoons butter, softened

12 cups water

1/2 cup baking soda

Coarse salt

1 For honey mustard, combine sour cream, mustard and honey in small bowl; whisk until smooth and well blended. Cover and refrigerate.

2 Dissolve yeast, sugar and 1/2 teaspoon salt in 1²/₃ cups warm water in large bowl of electric mixer; let stand 5 minutes or until bubbly.

3 Add flour and butter; beat with electric mixer at low speed until combined. Knead with dough hook at medium-low speed 5 minutes or until dough is smooth and elastic.

4 Shape dough into a ball. Place dough in greased bowl; turn to grease top. Cover and let rise in warm place 1 hour or until doubled in size.

5 Preheat oven to 450°F. Spray two baking sheets with nonstick cooking spray. Turn out dough onto floured surface. Divide dough into 12 pieces. Roll each piece into 12-inch-long rope. Cut each rope into eight pieces.

6 Bring 12 cups water to a boil in large saucepan; stir in baking soda until dissolved. Working in batches, drop dough pieces into boiling water; boil 30 seconds. Use slotted spoon to remove dough to prepared baking sheets. Sprinkle with coarse salt.

7 Bake 12 minutes or until dark golden brown, rotating baking sheets halfway through. Serve with honey mustard.

Cranberry Brie Bubble Bread

makes 12 servings

3 cups all-purpose flour

1 package (¹⁄₄ ounce) active dry yeast

1¹⁄₄ teaspoons salt, divided

1 cup warm water (120°F)

¹⁄₄ cup (¹⁄₂ stick) plus 2 tablespoons butter, melted, divided

³⁄₄ cup finely chopped pecans or walnuts

¹⁄₄ cup packed brown sugar

1 package (7 ounces) Brie cheese, cut into ¹⁄₄-inch pieces

1 cup whole-berry cranberry sauce

1 Combine flour, yeast and 1 teaspoon salt in large bowl of electric mixer. Stir in warm water and 2 tablespoons melted butter to form rough dough. Knead with dough hook at low speed 5 to 7 minutes or until dough is smooth and elastic.

2 Shape dough into a ball. Place in greased bowl; turn to grease top. Cover and let rise in warm place about 45 minutes or until doubled in size.

3 Spray 2-quart baking dish with nonstick cooking spray. Combine pecans, brown sugar and ¹⁄₄ teaspoon salt in shallow bowl; mix well. Place remaining ¹⁄₄ cup butter in another shallow bowl. Turn out dough onto floured surface; pat and stretch into 9×6-inch rectangle. Cut dough into 1-inch pieces; roll into balls.

4 Dip balls of dough in butter; roll in pecan mixture to coat. Place in prepared baking dish, layering with cheese and spoonfuls of cranberry sauce. Cover and let rise in warm place about 45 minutes or until dough is puffy. Preheat oven to 350°F.

5 Bake 30 minutes or until dough is firm and filling is bubbly. Cool on wire rack 15 to 20 minutes. Serve warm.

Tropical Banana Bread

makes 12 servings

1¹/₂ cups all-purpose flour

2¹/₂ teaspoons baking powder

¹/₂ teaspoon salt

6 tablespoons butter, softened

¹/₃ cup granulated sugar

¹/₃ cup packed brown sugar

2 eggs

3 ripe bananas, mashed

¹/₂ teaspoon vanilla

1 can (8 ounces) crushed pineapple, drained

¹/₃ cup flaked coconut

¹/₄ cup mini chocolate chips

¹/₃ cup chopped walnuts (optional)

1 Preheat oven to 350°F. Spray 9×5-inch loaf pan with nonstick cooking spray.

2 Whisk flour, baking powder and salt in small bowl. Beat butter, granulated sugar and brown sugar in large bowl with electric mixer at medium speed about 3 minutes or until light and fluffy. Add eggs one at a time, beating until well blended after each addition. Add bananas and vanilla; beat just until blended.

3 Gradually add flour mixture, beating just until blended. Fold in pineapple, coconut and chocolate chips. Spread batter in prepared pan; top with walnuts, if desired.

4 Bake 50 minutes or until toothpick inserted into center comes out with a few moist crumbs. Cool in pan 15 minutes. Remove to wire rack; cool completely.

Peanut Butter and Jelly Monkey Biscuits

makes 12 servings

¹/₄ cup creamy peanut butter

2 tablespoons butter

2¹/₄ cups all-purpose flour

¹/₄ cup sugar

1 tablespoon baking powder

¹/₂ teaspoon salt

¹/₄ cup (¹/₂ stick) cold butter, cut into small pieces

³/₄ cup buttermilk

6 tablespoons seedless strawberry jam, or favorite flavor

1 Preheat oven to 350°F. Line 9×5-inch loaf pan with foil, leaving 2-inch overhang on all sides. Spray foil with nonstick cooking spray.

2 Combine peanut butter and 2 tablespoons butter in small saucepan; cook and stir over low heat until melted. Cool slightly.

3 Whisk flour, sugar, baking powder and salt in medium bowl. Cut in ¹/₄ cup cold butter with pastry blender or fingertips until coarse crumbs form. Stir in buttermilk just until moistened.

4 Turn out dough onto lightly floured surface; knead 6 to 8 times. Pat dough into 8×6-inch rectangle; cut into 1-inch squares. Roll one third of squares in peanut butter mixture to coat; place in single layer in prepared pan. Top with 2 tablespoons jam, dropping by ¹/₂ teaspoonfuls evenly over squares. Repeat layers twice.

5 Bake 35 to 40 minutes or until jam is melted and bubbly and biscuits are flaky. Cool in pan on wire rack 10 minutes. Remove biscuits from pan using foil. Serve warm.

INDEX

INDEX

Metric Conversion Chart

VOLUME MEASUREMENTS (dry)

1/8 teaspoon = 0.5 mL
1/4 teaspoon = 1 mL
1/2 teaspoon = 2 mL
3/4 teaspoon = 4 mL
1 teaspoon = 5 mL
1 tablespoon = 15 mL
2 tablespoons = 30 mL
1/4 cup = 60 mL
1/3 cup = 75 mL
1/2 cup = 125 mL
2/3 cup = 150 mL
3/4 cup = 175 mL
1 cup = 250 mL
2 cups = 1 pint = 500 mL
3 cups = 750 mL
4 cups = 1 quart = 1 L

VOLUME MEASUREMENTS (fluid)

1 fluid ounce (2 tablespoons) = 30 mL
4 fluid ounces (1/2 cup) = 125 mL
8 fluid ounces (1 cup) = 250 mL
12 fluid ounces (1 1/2 cups) = 375 mL
16 fluid ounces (2 cups) = 500 mL

WEIGHTS (mass)

1/2 ounce = 15 g
1 ounce = 30 g
3 ounces = 90 g
4 ounces = 120 g
8 ounces = 225 g
10 ounces = 285 g
12 ounces = 360 g
16 ounces = 1 pound = 450 g

DIMENSIONS

1/16 inch = 2 mm
1/8 inch = 3 mm
1/4 inch = 6 mm
1/2 inch = 1.5 cm
3/4 inch = 2 cm
1 inch = 2.5 cm

OVEN TEMPERATURES

250°F = 120°C
275°F = 140°C
300°F = 150°C
325°F = 160°C
350°F = 180°C
375°F = 190°C
400°F = 200°C
425°F = 220°C
450°F = 230°C

BAKING PAN SIZES

Utensil	Size in Inches/Quarts	Metric Volume	Size in Centimeters
Baking or Cake Pan (square or rectangular)	8×8×2	2 L	20×20×5
	9×9×2	2.5 L	23×23×5
	12×8×2	3 L	30×20×5
	13×9×2	3.5 L	33×23×5
Loaf Pan	8×4×3	1.5 L	20×10×7
	9×5×3	2 L	23×13×7
Round Layer Cake Pan	8×1½	1.2 L	20×4
	9×1½	1.5 L	23×4
Pie Plate	8×1¼	750 mL	20×3
	9×1¼	1 L	23×3
Baking Dish or Casserole	1 quart	1 L	—
	1½ quart	1.5 L	—
	2 quart	2 L	—